vegetarian
meals

Published by:
TRIDENT REFERENCE PUBLISHING
801 12th Avenue South, Suite 400
Naples, Fl 34102 USA

Tel: + 1 (239) 649-7077
www.tridentreference.com
email: sales@tridentreference.com

vegetarian

meals

Vegetarian Meals
© TRIDENT REFERENCE PUBLISHING

Publisher
Simon St. John Bailey

Editor-in-chief
Susan Knightley

Prepress
Precision Prep & Press

All rights reserved. No part of this book may
be stored, reproduced or transmitted in any
form and by any means without written
permission of the Publisher, except in the
case of brief quotations embodied in critical
articles and reviews.

Includes Index
ISBN 1582796556
UPC 6 15269 96556 6

Printed in The United States

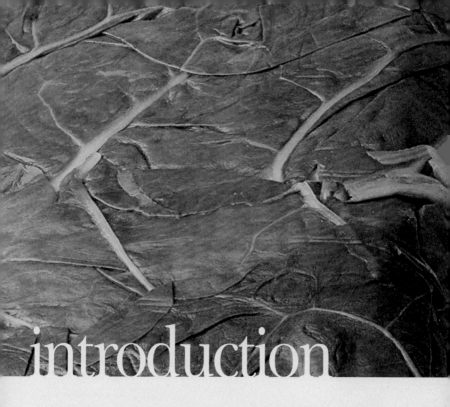

introduction

Vegetables are an essential part of a healthy diet; as well as their nutritional value –they are rich in fibers, minerals, vitamins and oligoelements– they add texture, flavor and color to dishes. Combining them with cereals and flours, millions of original and fun dishes can be made.

vegetarian meals
introduction

Nutrition and energy

Green or yellow vegetables have high levels
of vitamin A.
All vegetables are rich in vitamin C, many
of the B group and minerals.
Vegetable juices (carrot, tomato, celery)
energize and nourish very quickly because the
organism assimilates them immediately.

How to buy them?

- **Vegetables** (carrots, potatoes, tomatoes,
  beetroot, pumpkins, eggplants, zucchini,
  artichokes) have to show a clean, firm and
  stain-free surface. When soft or wrinkled,
  they are old.
- **Greens** (lettuce, endives, rocket, water
  cress, spinach) should have healthy,
  shiny leaves with no yellow or broken parts.
- **Cabbages** (cabbage, Brussels sprouts,
  cauliflower, broccoli) should be compact
  with no stains or bruises. Flowered broccoli
  are old.

- **Alliaceous vegetables** (garlic, onions, spring onions, leeks, chives, shallots) are rich in extremely volatile essential oils that give them their characteristic aroma and flavor. They should be absolutely fresh.
- **Herbs** (basil, dill, thyme, mint, marjoram, sage, parsley, coriander, tarragon, rosemary). When they are fresh not only give flavor and aroma to stews, salads, stuffings and sauces but also enrich food with their virtues. They are digestive and carminative.

The secret is how they are prepared

Winter tomatoes, that have a tougher skin, must be blanched in boiling water and then peeled.
If cucumbers, zucchini or carrots are to be eaten raw, it is best to scrub them well to remove impurities from the skin.
Greens have to be washed extremely carefully, leaf by leaf. If they are to be eaten in a salad, it is best to soak them in water and lemon juice for 30 minutes.

Difficulty scale

■□□ I Easy to do

■■□ I Requires attention

■■■ I Requires experience

ratatouille
kebabs

■■□ | Cooking time: 15 minutes - Preparation time: 30 minutes

ingredients

> 250 g/8 oz small pickling onions
> 1 small eggplant, cut into 2 cm/3/4 in cubes
> 1 red pepper, seeded and cut into 2 cm/3/4 in squares
> 4 zucchini, cut into 2 cm/3/4 in pieces
> 250 g/8 oz cherry tomatoes
> 250 g/8 oz button mushrooms

herb marinade

> 2 cloves garlic, crushed
> 2 small fresh red chilies, chopped
> 2 tablespoons chopped fresh basil
> 1 tablespoon chopped fresh oregano
> 1/2 cup/125 ml/4 fl oz olive oil
> 1/3 cup/90 ml/3 fl oz red wine

method

1. Cook onions in a saucepan of boiling water for 5 minutes. Drain, cool and cut into halves.
2. To make marinade, place garlic, chilies, basil, oregano, oil and wine in a bowl and mix to combine. Add onions, eggplant, red pepper, zucchini, tomatoes and mushrooms, toss to coat and marinate at room temperature for at least 1 hour.
3. Drain vegetables and reserve marinade. Thread vegetables onto lightly oiled skewers and cook on a preheated hot barbecue grill, basting occasionally with marinade, for 4-5 minutes each side, or until cooked.

....
Serves 8

tip from the chef

Try a delicious variation serving these kebabs with Provençal relish (combine mayonnaise with chopped garlic and parsley).

red lentil
felafel with dip

■ ■ □ | Cooking time: 30 minutes - Preparation time: 40 minutes

method

1. Place lentils and 4 cups/1 liter/1³/₄ pt water in a saucepan and bring to the boil over a medium heat. Reduce heat and simmer, stirring occasionally, for 15-20 minutes or until lentils are tender and liquid is absorbed – there should be about 4 cups/1 liter/1³/₄ pt cooked lentils. Set aside to cool.

2. Place lentils, breadcrumbs, onion, chilies, parsley, garlic, cumin and eggs in a food processor and process until a soft ball forms. Take 2 tablespoons of mixture and shape into flat balls.

3. Heat oil in a large saucepan until a cube of bread dropped in browns in 50 seconds, then deep-fry felafel, a few at a time, for 4 minutes or until brown. Drain on absorbent kitchen paper.

4. To make dip, place mint, cumin, chili powder, yogurt and lemon juice in a bowl and mix to combine. Serve with felafel.

....
Makes 24

ingredients

> **500 g/1 lb red lentils**
> **2 cups/125 g/4 oz breadcrumbs, made from stale bread**
> **1 onion, chopped**
> **4 dried red chilies, crushed**
> **4 tablespoons chopped fresh parsley**
> **1 clove garlic, crushed**
> **2 teaspoons ground cumin**
> **2 eggs**
> **vegetable oil for deep-frying**

minty yogurt dip

> **2 tablespoons shredded fresh mint**
> **1 teaspoon ground cumin**
> **¹/₂ teaspoon chili powder**
> **1 cup/200 g/6¹/₂ oz natural yogurt**
> **2 tablespoons lemon juice**

tip from the chef

For a light meal, place felafel on flat bread, top with shredded lettuce, chopped tomatoes and finely sliced onions, then drizzle with the dip and roll up.

broccoli
and cashew fritters

■□□ I Cooking time: 5 minutes - Preparation time: 20 minutes

method

1. Sift flour, garam masala, cumin, ground coriander and curry, baking and chili powders together into a bowl. Stir in water and oil and mix to make a smooth batter. Add cashews, spring onions and fresh coriander and mix to combine.

2. Heat oil in a large saucepan over a high heat until a cube of bread dropped in browns in 50 seconds. Dip broccoli into batter and deep-fry, in batches, for 3-5 minutes or until golden. Drain on absorbent kitchen paper.

3. To make chutney, place onion, chilies, mint leaves, ginger, chutney and lemon juice in a food processor and process to combine. Serve with fritters.

Serves 6

ingredients

> 1 cup/125 g/4 oz chickpea flour
> 1 teaspoon garam masala
> 1 teaspoon ground cumin
> 1 teaspoon ground coriander
> 1 teaspoon curry powder
> 1/2 teaspoon baking powder
> 1/2 teaspoon chili powder
> 1 cup/250 ml/8 fl oz water
> 2 tablespoons vegetable oil
> 125 g/4 oz cashews, chopped
> 4 spring onions, finely chopped
> 3 tablespoons chopped fresh coriander
> vegetable oil for deep-frying
> 1 kg/2 lb broccoli florets

mango mint chutney

> 1 onion, chopped
> 3 fresh green chilies, chopped
> 1 bunch fresh mint
> 1 tablespoon finely grated fresh ginger
> 1/2 cup/155 g/5 oz mango chutney
> 2 tablespoons lemon juice

tip from the chef

Chickpea flour is used extensively in Indian cooking and is available from Oriental food stores and some supermarkets. Alternatively, you can make your own by lightly roasting uncooked chickpeas, then using a food processor or blender, grind them to make a flour.

tofu
vegetable laksa

■■□ | Cooking time: 30 minutes - Preparation time: 20 minutes

ingredients

> **2 tablespoons peanut oil**
> **6 kaffir lime leaves, finely shredded**
> **1 tablespoon palm or brown sugar**
> **2 cups/500 ml/16 fl oz vegetable stock**
> **2 cups/500 ml/16 fl oz coconut cream**
> **250 g/8 oz firm tofu, cut into 1 cm/1/2 in thick slices**
> **1 bunch/500 g/1 lb baby bok choy, leaves separated**
> **90 g/3 oz fresh or canned baby sweet corn, halved**
> **1 red pepper, sliced**
> **250 g/8 oz fresh egg or rice noodles, soaked in boiling water for 2 minutes**
> **60 g/2 oz bean sprouts**
> **3 tablespoons fresh coriander leaves**

spice paste

> **4 small fresh red chilies, chopped**
> **5 spring onions, finely chopped**
> **1 tablespoon finely chopped fresh lemon grass, or 1/4 teaspoon dried lemon grass, soaked in hot water until soft**
> **1 tablespoon grated fresh ginger**
> **1 tablespoon finely grated fresh or bottled galanga (optional)**
> **1 teaspoon ground turmeric**
> **1 teaspoon peanut oil**

method

1. To make paste, place chilies, spring onions, lemon grass, ginger, galanga (if using), turmeric and oil in a food processor or blender and process to make smooth paste.
2. Heat the 2 tablespoons of oil in a heavy-based saucepan over a medium heat, add spice paste and cook, stirring, for 5 minutes or until fragrant.
3. Stir in lime leaves, sugar, stock and coconut cream, bring to simmering and simmer for 15-20 minutes.
4. Add tofu, bok choy, sweet corn and red pepper and cook for 3 minutes or until bok choy is bright green and tofu is heated.
5. To serve, divide noodles between soup bowls, ladle over soup and garnish with bean sprouts and coriander.

....

Serves 4

tip from the chef

Laksa paste and powder are available from Oriental food stores and some supermarkets and may be used in place of the spice paste in this recipe.

tomato
and ricotta panini

■□□ | Cooking time: 40 minutes - Preparation time: 25 minutes

method

1. Place tomatoes, cut side up, on a baking tray, sprinkle with a little oil and bake at 200°C/400°F/Gas 6 for 35 minutes or until soft.
2. Place ricotta cheese, basil, black peppercorns and chili sauce in a bowl and mix to combine. Spread ricotta mixture over the bases of the bread rounds, then top with roasted tomatoes and spinach leaves and cover with bread tops. Brush sandwiches with oil, place in a preheated frying pan and cook over a low heat for 2-3 minutes each side or until golden and warmed through.

ingredients

> 6 plum (egg or Italian) tomatoes, halved lengthwise
> olive oil
> 315 g/10 oz ricotta cheese, drained
> 2 tablespoons chopped fresh basil
> 2 teaspoons crushed black peppercorns
> 1 tablespoon hot chili sauce
> 4 Turkish (pide) bread rounds, split
> 125 g/4 oz baby spinach leaves

....
Serves 4

tip from the chef

Turkish bread (pide) is a flat white leavened bread similar to Italian flatbread. It is usually baked in ovals measuring 30-40 cm/12-16 in or sometimes as 10 cm/4 in rounds. If Turkish bread (pide) is unavailable, country-style Italian bread, rye bread, sour dough, ciabatta or focaccia could be used instead.

endive
and goat's cheese salad

■□□ | Cooking time: 7 minutes - Preparation time: 5 minutes

ingredients
> **8 thick slices goat's cheese**
> **1 tablespoon olive oil**
> **freshly ground black pepper**
> **300 g/9½ oz curly endive leaves**
> **250 g/8 oz cherry tomatoes, halved**
> **1 cucumber, sliced**
> **1 small French stick, sliced and toasted**
> **2 tablespoons white wine vinegar**

method
1. Brush goat's cheese with oil and season with black pepper. Place under a preheated medium grill and cook for 3 minutes each side or until golden.
2. Arrange endive leaves, tomatoes, cucumber, toast and goat's cheese on a serving platter. Drizzle with vinegar and serve immediately.

....
Serves 4

tip from the chef
A simple yet delicious salad with a strong Mediterranean influence. Curly endive is a member of the chicory family and has a more bitter taste than lettuce.

raw
mushroom salad

■ ☐ ☐ | Cooking time: 0 minute - Preparation time: 15 minutes

method

1. Place mushrooms in a bowl. To make marinade, combine oil, lemon juice, vinegar, garlic and chili powder in a screw-top jar. Shake well and pour over mushrooms. Toss and leave to marinate for 2-3 hours, tossing from time to time.
2. Gently fold through chives, parsley and red pepper and serve.

Serves 6

ingredients

> 500 g/1 lb button mushrooms, thinly sliced
> 1 tablespoon finely chopped fresh chives
> 1 tablespoon finely chopped fresh parsley
> 1/2 red pepper, diced

marinade

> 1/2 cup/125 ml/4 fl oz olive oil
> 3 tablespoons lemon juice
> 1 tablespoon white wine vinegar
> 1 clove garlic, crushed
> 1/4 teaspoon chili powder

tip from the chef

An all-time favorite, this mushroom salad is easy to make and delicious served as part of a salad buffet.

roasted
peppers with herbs

■ ■ □ | Cooking time: 20 minutes - Preparation time: 25 minutes

method

1. Place red and green peppers and chilies in a hot frying pan (a) or comal and cook until skins are blistered and charred. Place peppers and chilies in a plastic food bag (b) and stand for 10 minutes or until cool enough to handle.
2. Carefully remove skins (c) from peppers and chilies, then cut off tops and remove seeds and membranes. Cut into thick slices.
3. Place onions in frying pan or comal and cook for 5 minutes or until soft and charred.
4. Place peppers, chilies, onions, marjoram, thyme, lime juice, oil and black pepper to taste in a bowl and toss to combine. Stand for 30 minutes before serving.

ingredients

- > 3 red peppers
- > 2 green peppers
- > 4 medium fresh green chilies
- > 2 onions, quartered
- > 2 tablespoons fresh marjoram leaves
- > 2 tablespoons fresh thyme leaves
- > 1/4 cup/60 ml/2 fl oz lime juice
- > 1/4 cup/60 ml/2 fl oz olive oil
- > freshly ground black pepper

....

Serves 6

tip from the chef

A comal is a steel, cast iron or unglazed earthenware cooking disk, which is used for cooking and heating tortillas and for toasting other ingredients such as chilies and pumpkin seeds.

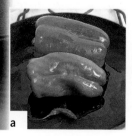

a

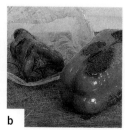

b

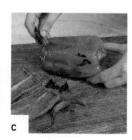

c

spicy
vegetable pies

■■☐ | Cooking time: 60 minutes - Preparation time: 45 minutes

method

1. Roll out pastry to 3 mm/1/8 in thick and use to line six 1 cup/250 ml/8 fl oz capacity pie dishes. Chill.
2. Boil, steam or microwave sweet potatoes until soft. Drain and place in a bowl. Add milk and mash, then stir in ricotta cheese.
3. Boil, steam or microwave carrots until soft. Drain and add to sweet potato mixture. Add cauliflower, beans, red pepper, chives, ginger and black pepper to taste and mix to combine.
4. Divide vegetable mixture between pastry cases, sprinkle with Parmesan cheese and bake at 200°C/400°F/Gas 6 for 30 minutes or until pastry is golden and filling cooked.

....
Serves 6

ingredients

> **350 g/11 oz prepared shortcrust pastry**
> **500 g/1 lb chopped sweet potatoes**
> **1/2 cup/125 ml/4 fl oz milk**
> **125 g/4 oz ricotta cheese, drained**
> **315 g/10 oz chopped carrots**
> **185 g/6 oz cauliflower, chopped**
> **125 g/4 oz green beans, halved**
> **1 red pepper, chopped**
> **3 tablespoons snipped fresh chives**
> **1 tablespoon finely grated fresh ginger**
> **freshly ground black pepper**
> **60 g/2 oz grated Parmesan cheese**

tip from the chef

The pies may also be filled with a mixture of blanched spinach, drained and finely chopped, cottage cheese, grated Moliterno cheese, nutmeg and chopped walnuts. The Moliterno can be replaced with a fine hard cheese with pepper.

vegetables
in pitta baskets

■■□ | Cooking time: 35 minutes - Preparation time: 35 minutes

method

1. Heat oil in a wok or large saucepan until a cube of bread dropped in browns in 50 seconds. Cook pitta breads one at a time, pressing with the head of a metal soup ladle to form a basket. Drain on absorbent kitchen paper. Set aside and keep warm.
2. To make filling, boil, steam or microwave potatoes, carrot, zucchini, snow peas and squash, separately, until tender. Set aside and keep warm.
3. Place ginger, honey, orange juice, nuts and chives in a large bowl and mix to combine. Add warm vegetables and toss to coat. Spoon vegetable mixture into warm baskets and serve immediately.

....
Serves 4

ingredients

> **vegetable oil for deep frying**
> **2 large pitta bread rounds, split through center**

vegetable filling

> **8 baby new potatoes, cut into bite-sized pieces**
> **1 carrot, chopped**
> **1 zucchini, chopped**
> **250 g/8 oz snow peas**
> **250 g/8 oz green or yellow baby squash, quartered**
> **1 tablespoon grated fresh ginger**
> **2 tablespoons honey**
> **2 tablespoons orange juice**
> **2 tablespoons chopped macadamia or Brazil nuts**
> **2 tablespoons snipped fresh chives**

tip from the chef

These pitta baskets make wonderful containers for serving all kinds of food. You might like to try them with curried vegetables.

ginger sweet potato quiche

■ ■ □ | Cooking time: 60 minutes - Preparation time: 30 minutes

ingredients

> **200 g/6¹/2 oz prepared shortcrust pastry**

sweet potato filling

> **1 kg/2 lb sweet potatoes, peeled and chopped**
> **30 g/1 oz butter**
> **1 fresh red chili, chopped**
> **1 tablespoon finely grated fresh ginger**
> **2 teaspoons ground cumin**
> **1 cup/250 g/8 oz sour cream**
> **3 eggs, lightly beaten**
> **2 tablespoons chopped fresh coriander leaves**

method

1. Roll out pastry to 3 mm/¹/8 in thick and use to line a greased, deep 23 cm/9 in tart tin. Chill for 30 minutes, then prick base and sides of pastry case with a fork, line with nonstick baking paper and fill with uncooked rice. Bake at 200°C/400°F/Gas 6 for 6 minutes, then remove rice and paper and bake for 4 minutes longer or until pastry is lightly browned. Set aside to cool.
3. To make filling, boil, steam or microwave sweet potatoes until tender. Cool slightly. Melt butter in a saucepan over a medium heat, add chili, ginger and cumin and cook for 1 minute. Set aside.
4. Place sweet potatoes, sour cream and eggs in a food processor and process until smooth. Stir in chili mixture and coriander.
5. Pour filling into pastry case, reduce oven temperature to 180°C/350°F/Gas 4 and bake for 35-40 minutes or until filling is set.

....

Serves 6

tip from the chef

Fresh root ginger freezes well. When you want to use it, simply grate the required amount off the frozen piece. A small Oriental ginger grater is an inexpensive and worthwhile investment.

puff mushroom pizza

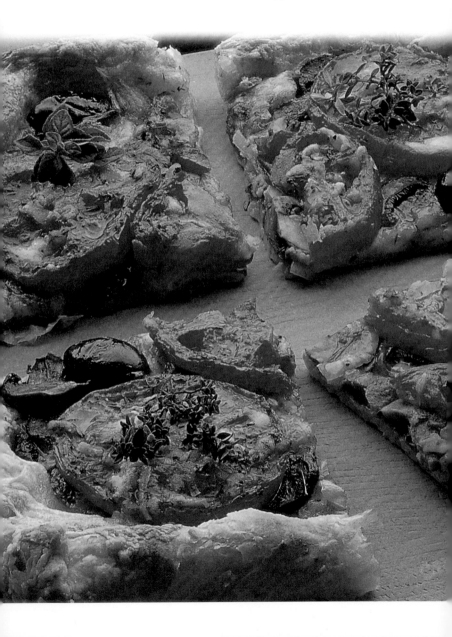

■■□ I Cooking time: 30 minutes - Preparation time: 35 minutes

method

1. Roll out pastry to fit a greased 26 x 32 cm/10½ x 12¾ in Swiss roll tin.
2. Sprinkle pastry with Parmesan cheese and mozzarella cheese, then top with onion, mushrooms, tomatoes and olives. Sprinkle with oregano and thyme and bake at 200°C/400°F/Gas 6 for 30 minutes or until pastry is puffed and golden. Serve hot, warm or cold.

....

Serves 6

ingredients

> 375 g/12 oz prepared puff pastry
> 60 g/2 oz grated Parmesan cheese
> 125 g/4 oz grated mozzarella cheese
> 1 onion, thinly sliced
> 200 g/6½ oz mushrooms, sliced
> 3 tomatoes, cut into 1 cm/½ in slices
> 10 pitted black olives
> 2 teaspoons chopped fresh oregano or ½ teaspoon dried oregano
> 2 teaspoons chopped fresh thyme or ½ teaspoon dried thyme

tip from the chef

This quick pastry-based pizza is great for weekend meals and leftovers are ideal for packed lunches.

garden pizza

■□□ | Cooking time: 15 minutes - Preparation time: 35 minutes

ingredients
> 1 ready-made pizza base

garden topping
> 250 g/8 oz asparagus spears, cut into 4 cm/1 1/2 in pieces
> 125 g/4 oz baby yellow squash or zucchini, sliced
> 3 spring onions, chopped
> 155 g/5 oz broccoli, cut into florets
> 125 g/4 oz small peas
> 2 tablespoons chopped fresh basil or 1 teaspoon dried basil
> 60 g/2 oz grated mozzarella cheese
> 60 g/2 oz grated Parmesan cheese
> freshly ground black pepper

method
1. Place pizza base on a lightly greased baking tray.
2. Arrange asparagus, squash or zucchini, spring onions, broccoli, peas and basil over dough. Sprinkle with mozzarella cheese, Parmesan cheese and black pepper to taste.
3. Bake at 200°C/400°F/Gas 6 for 10-15 minutes or until cheese is golden and base is crisp.

....
Serves 4

tip from the chef
Remember that pizzas do not have to be large and round. Some are rectangles, some oval, some small individual circles and some have a deep crust and sides more resembling a pie (which, after all, is what pizza means in Italian).

spinach
pancakes

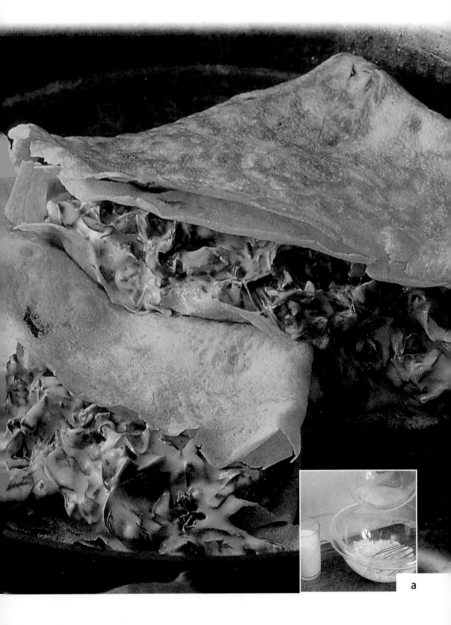

a

■■□ I Cooking time: 35 minutes - Preparation time: 30 minutes

method

1. To make pancakes, boil or microwave spinach or silverbeet until wilted. Drain and squeeze out as much liquid as possible.
2. Place flour in a bowl and make a well in the center. Add eggs and a little of the milk (a) and beat working in all the flour. Beat in butter and remaining milk, then stir through spinach (b).
3. Pour 2-3 tablespoons of batter into a 20 cm/8 in nonstick frying pan and tilt pan so batter evenly covers base. Cook for 1 minute each side (c) or until lightly browned. Set aside and keep warm. Repeat with remaining batter.
4. To make filling, heat oil in a frying pan, add garlic and cook over a medium heat, stirring, for 1 minute. Add spinach or silverbeet and cook for 3 minutes longer or until spinach or silverbeet wilts.
5. Stir in sour cream or yogurt and black pepper to taste. Spread a spoonful of filling over each pancake. Fold pancakes into quarters and serve immediately.

ingredients

> 8 spinach or silverbeet leaves, shredded
> 1 cup/125 g/4 oz flour
> 4 eggs, lightly beaten
> 155 ml/5 fl oz milk
> 30 g/1 oz butter, melted

spinach filling

> 2 teaspoons vegetable oil
> 2 cloves garlic, crushed
> 12 spinach or silverbeet leaves, shredded
> 300 g/9 1/2 oz sour cream or natural yogurt
> freshly ground black pepper

Serves 6

b   c

tip from the chef

These wholesome pancakes envelop a delicious savory filling and are best served immediately after cooking.

curry vegetable pancakes

■■□ I Cooking time: 55 minutes - Preparation time: 45 minutes

ingredients

> 1 tablespoon vegetable oil
> 1 leek, cut into thin strips
> 1 carrot, cut into thin strips
> 250 g/8 oz broccoli florets
> 315 g/10 oz canned butter beans, rinsed and drained

pasta and polenta pancakes

> 75 g/2¹/2 oz tiny dried pasta shapes, such as risoni or orzo, anellini, ditalini or conchigliette
> ¹/2 cup/90 g/3 oz polenta
> ³/4 cup/185 ml/6 fl oz boiling water
> ¹/2 cup/125 ml/4 fl oz milk
> 1 egg, lightly beaten
> ³/4 cup/90 g/3 oz flour
> butter

coconut curry sauce

> 15 g/¹/2 oz butter
> 1 tablespoon curry powder or curry paste
> 1 teaspoon finely grated fresh ginger
> ¹/4 teaspoon ground turmeric
> 1¹/2 cups/375 ml/12 fl oz coconut cream
> 1 tablespoon chopped fresh coriander

method

1. To make pancakes, cook pasta in boiling water in a large saucepan following packet directions. Drain and rinse under cold running water. Drain again and set aside. Place polenta in a large bowl and stir in boiling water. Cover and set aside for 15 minutes.

2. Add milk, egg, flour and pasta to polenta mixture and mix well to combine. Melt a little butter in a frying pan over a low heat and when butter starts to foam, pour ¹/4 cup/60 ml/2 fl oz batter into pan and cook for 2 minutes or until golden, turn over and cook for 2 minutes longer. Remove pancake, set aside and keep warm. Repeat with remaining batter.

3. To make sauce, heat butter in a frying pan over a medium heat, add curry powder or paste, ginger and turmeric and cook, stirring, for 2 minutes. Stir in coconut cream and coriander, bring to simmering and simmer for 1-2 minutes.

4. Heat oil in a wok or frying pan over a medium heat, add leek and stir-fry for 1-2 minutes or until just tender. Add carrot and broccoli and stir-fry for 4-5 minutes longer or until vegetables are just tender. Add beans and cook for 1-2 minutes or until heated through.

5. To assemble, place a pancake on each serving plate, top with vegetable mixture, then with a second pancake. Spoon over sauce and serve immediately.

Serves 4-6

tip from the chef

If coconut cream is unavailable, substitute with coconut milk. Although coconut cream is thicker than coconut milk, they are interchangeable in recipes. Both products can be purchased canned, as a long-life product in cartons or as a powder to which you add water. Once opened, they have a short life and should be used within a day or so.

bean
sprout omelette

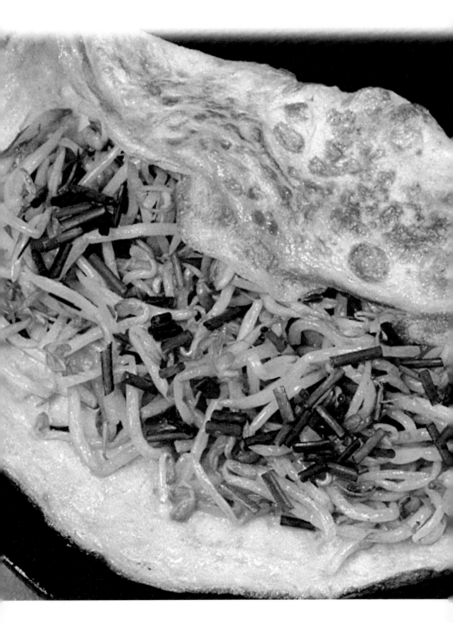

■□□ | Cooking time: 5 minutes - Preparation time: 5 minutes

method

1. To make filling, melt butter in a small frying pan. Add ginger, bean sprouts and chives and cook for 1 minute. Remove from pan and keep warm.
2. To make omelette, melt butter in a small frying pan. Lightly whisk together eggs and water and season with pepper. Pour into pan and cook over medium heat.
Continually draw the edge of the omelette in with a fork (a) during cooking until no liquid remains and the omelette is lightly set.
3. Sprinkle the bean sprout mixture over the omelette and fold in half. Slip onto a plate (b) and serve immediately.

....
Serves 1

ingredients

filling
> **30 g/1 oz butter**
> **2 tablespoons grated fresh ginger**
> **4 tablespoons bean sprouts**
> **4 chives, finely chopped**

omelette
> **1 teaspoon butter**
> **2 eggs**
> **2 teaspoons water**
> **freshly ground black pepper**

a

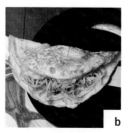

b

tip from the chef
For a fragrant-flavored omelette, add 2 tablespoons snipped fresh chives to the beaten eggs.

vegetable
frittata wedges

■ ■ □ | Cooking time: 45 minutes - Preparation time: 35 minutes

ingredients

> **2 tablespoons vegetable oil**
> **1 onion, very thinly sliced**
> **1 potato, very thinly sliced**
> **350 g/11 oz canned asparagus spears, drained**
> **1 red pepper, cut into long strips**
> **1 zucchini, cut into long strips**
> **6 eggs, beaten**
> **freshly ground black pepper**
> **2 tablespoons grated Parmesan cheese**

method

1. Drizzle oil over the base of a 23 cm/9 in quiche dish, then spread with onions and top with potato slices. Cover dish with aluminum foil and bake at 180°C/350°F/Gas 4 for 30 minutes or until potato is tender.
2. Arrange asparagus spears and red pepper and zucchini strips like the spokes of a wheel onto top of potato, then pour over eggs and season with black pepper to taste. Scatter with Parmesan cheese.
3. Bake, covered, for 15 minutes or until frittata is firm. Cool for 10 minutes, then cut into wedges and serve.

....

Makes 8

tip from the chef
For this frittata, when fresh asparagus are off season, use small artichoke stems, boiled and cut in thin slices.

vegetable
pilaf with almonds

■■□ | Cooking time: 40 minutes - Preparation time: 40 minutes

method

1. Heat oil in large saucepan, cook onion (a) 5 minutes, stirring occasionally. Add garlic, almonds and rice (b), cook, stirring, 2 minutes.
2. Add vegetables, currants, orange rind, orange juice (c), water and bay leaf. Bring to the boil, simmer, covered, 30 minutes or until rice is cooked.
3. Add tamari, cook covered further 5 minutes. Remove bay leaf before serving.

....

Serves 4

ingredients

> 2 tablespoons olive oil
> 1 onion, chopped
> 1 clove garlic, crushed
> 1/4 cup almonds
> 2 cups long grain brown rice
> 1 stick celery, chopped
> 125 g/4 oz green beans, chopped
> 125 g/4 oz zucchini, chopped
> 125 g/4 oz broccoli florets
> 1 small green pepper, chopped
> 2 tablespoons currants
> 2 tablespoons grated orange rind
> juice of 1 orange
> 600 ml/1 pt boiling water
> 1 bay leaf
> 7 tablespoons tamari

tip from the chef

The secret of good pilaf is in the rice cooking, that must be al dente, never chewy or sticky. As vegetables provide liquid to the cooking, it's better not to add too much water.

a

b

c

rice and
hummus terrine

■ ■ ■ | Cooking time: 25 minutes - Preparation time: 45 minutes

ingredients
> 500 g/1 lb spinach, stalks removed
> 4 zucchini, sliced
> 4 carrots, sliced
> 2 avocados, stoned, peeled and mashed
> 3 tablespoons mayonnaise
> 1 tablespoon lemon juice
> 1 cup/220 g/7 oz rice, cooked
> 3 red peppers, halved, roasted and skins removed, chopped
> 200 g/6 1/2 oz hummus

method
1. Line an 11 x 21 cm/4 1/2 x 8 1/2 in loaf tin with plastic food wrap. Set aside.
2. Boil, steam or microwave spinach leaves until just wilted. Drain well. Line prepared loaf tin with overlapping spinach leaves. Allow leaves to overhang the sides of the tin.
3. Boil, steam or microwave zucchini and carrots, separately, until just tender. Drain and set aside.
4. Place avocados, mayonnaise and lemon juice in a bowl and mix to combine. Set aside.
5. Pack half the rice into spinach-lined loaf tin, pressing down well with the back of a spoon. Top with half the red peppers, zucchini, carrots and hummus. Spread with avocado mixture, then top with remaining rice, red peppers, zucchini, carrots and, lastly, hummus.
6. Fold overhanging spinach leaves over filling. Place a heavy weight on terrine and refrigerate for at least 4 hours before serving. To serve, unmold and cut into slices.

....
Serves 6-8

tip from the chef
Hummus is a popular Middle Eastern dip made from a purée of cooked chickpeas and tahini (sesame paste).

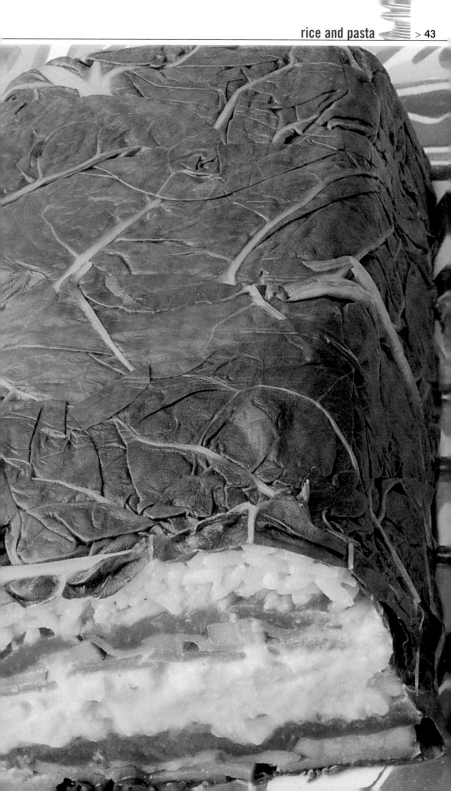

noodles
with bok choy sauce

■□□ I Cooking time: 25 minutes - Preparation time: 15 minutes

method

1. Cook noodles in boiling water in a large saucepan, following packet directions. Drain, set aside and keep warm.
2. To make sauce, heat oil in a wok or frying pan over a high heat, add bok choy and stir-fry for 2-3 minutes. Add soy sauce, sesame oil, kechap manis, chili sauce and ginger. Bring to a simmer and cook for 1 minute.
3. Add tofu and bean sprouts and stir-fry for 2-3 minutes or until heated through. Add noodles to pan and toss to combine. Serve immediately.

....

Serves 4

ingredients

> **250 g/8 oz quick-cooking noodles**

bok choy sauce

> **1 tablespoon vegetable oil**
> **2 bunches/500 g/1 lb baby bok choy, leaves separated and trimmed**
> **1/3 cup/90 ml/3 fl oz soy sauce**
> **2 tablespoons sesame oil**
> **2 tablespoons kechap manis**
> **2 tablespoons sweet chili sauce**
> **2 tablespoons pickled ginger**
> **315 g/10 oz tofu, cut into 1 cm/1/2 in cubes**
> **150 g/5 oz bean sprouts**

tip from the chef

These noodles, a classic of Japanese cuisine, can also be combined with bean sprouts, sliced mushrooms, shredded carrots, chives and grated ginger.

grilled
vegetable pasta

■■□ | Cooking time: 30 minutes - Preparation time: 40 minutes

ingredients

> 1 red pepper, seeded and cut into quarters
> 1 yellow pepper, seeded and cut into quarters
> 1 green pepper, seeded and cut into quarters
> 6 baby eggplant, cut lengthwise into quarters
> 2 tablespoons olive oil
> 8 plum (egg or Italian) tomatoes, halved
> 1 red onion, sliced
> 2 cloves garlic, crushed
> 1 tablespoon chopped fresh purple basil or green basil
> freshly ground black pepper
> 500 g/1 lb fresh spinach tagliatelle

tip from the chef

This pretty pasta dish is delightful for casual entertaining. A complete meal might start with a mixed green salad and crusty bread and finish with a selection of fresh seasonal fruit. If plum (egg or Italian) tomatoes are unavailable, use small ordinary tomatoes instead.

method

1. Place red, yellow and green pepper quarters, skin side up, under a preheated hot grill and cook for 5-10 minutes until skins are blistered and charred. Place peppers in a plastic food bag and set aside until cool enough to handle. Remove skins from peppers and cut flesh into thick slices.
2. Brush cut surfaces of eggplant lightly with oil and cook under preheated hot grill for 2-3 minutes each side or until golden.
3. Place tomatoes, skin side down, under preheated hot grill and cook for 2 minutes or until soft.
4. Heat remaining oil in a frying pan over a medium heat, add onion and garlic and cook, stirring, for 4 minutes or until onion is soft and golden. Add red pepper, yellow pepper, green pepper, eggplant, tomatoes, basil and black pepper to taste and cook, stirring, for 4 minutes.
5. Cook pasta in boiling water in a large saucepan following packet directions. Drain well and top with vegetable mixture. Serve immediately.

....

Serves 4

crispy noodles and vegetables

■■□ | Cooking time: 25 minutes - Preparation time: 20 minutes

method

1. Cook noodles in boiling water in a large saucepan for 2-3 minutes, drain and dry on absorbent kitchen paper. Heat oil in a large saucepan over a medium heat until a cube of bread dropped in browns in 50 seconds. Deep-fry noodles, in batches, for 2-3 minutes or until puffed and crispy. Drain on absorbent kitchen paper, set aside and keep warm.

2. Cook mixed vegetables following packet directions. Drain, set aside and keep warm.

3. To make sauce, place peanut butter, sugar, garlic, coconut milk, soy sauce and chili sauce in a saucepan and cook over a low heat, stirring, for 3-5 minutes or until hot. To serve, divide noodles between serving plates, top with vegetables and sauce.

ingredients

> **315 g/10 oz fresh thin egg noodles**
> **vegetable oil for deep-frying**
> **500 g/1 lb packaged frozen Chinese stir-fry mixed vegetables**

peanut sauce

> **3/4 cup/200 g/6 1/2 oz crunchy peanut butter**
> **1 tablespoon brown sugar**
> **1 clove garlic, crushed**
> **1 1/2 cups/375 ml/12 fl oz coconut milk**
> **2 tablespoons light soy sauce**
> **2 teaspoons hot chili sauce**

....
Serves 4

tip from the chef

When using cellophane noodles instead of egg noodles, cook in a wok in shallow canola or sunflower oil with a few drops of sesame oil, along with finely chopped vegetables. Cooking the pasta is practically instant.

pasta-topped
ratatouille

■ ■ ■ | Cooking time: 2 hours - Preparation time: 60 minutes

ingredients

pasta topping

> 315 g/10 oz small pasta shapes of your choice
> 90 g/3 oz butter, melted
> 45 g/1 1/2 oz grated fresh Parmesan cheese

bean ratatouille

> 2 small eggplant, sliced
> salt
> olive oil
> 1 large onion, thinly sliced
> 1 red pepper, sliced
> 1 green pepper, sliced
> 2 large zucchini, sliced
> 185 g/6 oz button mushrooms, sliced
> 500 g/1 lb tomatoes, sliced
> 315 g/10 oz canned three bean mix, rinsed and drained
> 1 clove garlic, crushed
> 1 teaspoon dried oregano leaves
> 1 teaspoon dried basil leaves
> 1/2 teaspoon chili paste (sambal oelek)
> 440 g/14 oz canned tomatoes, undrained and puréed
> 1/3 cup/90 ml/3 fl oz vegetable stock
> freshly ground black pepper

method

1. To make topping, cook pasta in boiling water in a large saucepan following packet directions. Drain, rinse under cold running water and drain again. Place pasta, butter and Parmesan cheese in a bowl and mix to combine. Set aside.

2. To make ratatouille, place eggplant in a colander, sprinkle with salt and set aside to drain for 30 minutes. Rinse eggplant under cold running water and pat dry with absorbent kitchen paper.

3. Heat 2 tablespoons oil in a frying pan over a medium heat and cook eggplant, in batches, for 3-4 minutes on each side or until soft. Drain on absorbent kitchen paper. Cook onion, red pepper, green pepper, zucchini and mushrooms separately in the same way, adding more oil as necessary.

4. Arrange eggplant slices, onion, red and green peppers, zucchini, mushrooms and tomatoes in layers in a large ovenproof dish. Place bean mix, garlic, oregano, basil, chili paste (sambal oelek), puréed tomatoes, stock and black pepper to taste in a large bowl and mix to combine. Pour bean mixture over vegetables and bake at 180°C/350°F/Gas 4 for 45 minutes.

5. Spoon topping over vegetables and bake for 20-30 minutes longer or until topping is golden and vegetables are tender.

....
Serves 8

tip from the chef

Any small pasta shape such as fusilli (spirals or twists), farfalle (butterflies or bow ties), conchiglie (medium-size shells), dried gnocchi or small elbow (short-cut) macaroni is suitable for this recipe.

Canned three bean mix as used in this recipe is a mixture of butter beans, red kidney beans and lima beans. Any canned mixed beans are suitable to use.

rigatoni
with pumpkin

■□□ | Cooking time: 20 minutes - Preparation time: 10 minutes

method

1. Cook rigatoni in boiling water in a large saucepan, following packet directions. Drain, set aside and keep warm.
2. Melt 60 g/2 oz butter in a large saucepan and cook pumpkin over a medium heat for 5-10 minutes or until tender.
3. Stir chives, nutmeg, Parmesan cheese, black pepper to taste, rigatoni and remaining butter into pumpkin mixture and toss to combine. Serve immediately.

ingredients

> 500 g/1 lb rigatoni
> 90 g/3 oz butter
> 250 g/8 oz pumpkin, cut into small cubes
> 1 tablespoon snipped fresh chives
> pinch ground nutmeg
> 30 g/1 oz grated fresh Parmesan cheese
> freshly ground black pepper

....
Serves 4

tip from the chef

Pumpkin goes well with all pasta varieties. Combine with a little ricotta cheese and grated Parmesan cheese to make great fillings for lasagna, cannelloni or ravioli.

vegetarian
lasagna

■■□ | Cooking time: 60 minutes - Preparation time: 45 minutes

ingredients

> 200 g/6¹/2 oz fresh
  lasagna sheets
> 185 g/6 oz grated tasty
  cheese (mature Cheddar)

tomato sauce

> 1 tablespoon olive oil
> 185 g/6 oz button
  mushrooms, sliced
> 1 onion, chopped
> 1 clove garlic, crushed
> 1 teaspoon seeded,
  chopped fresh red chili
> 3 zucchini, sliced
> 2 x 440 g/14 oz canned
  tomatoes, mashed
> ¹/2 cup/125 ml/4 fl oz
  white wine
> 2 tablespoons chopped
  fresh basil
> 2 tablespoons chopped
  fresh parsley

spinach and ricotta
sauce

> 250 g/8 oz frozen
  spinach, thawed and well
  drained
> 250 g/8 oz ricotta cheese,
  drained
> 1 egg, lightly beaten
> freshly ground black pepper

white sauce

> 60 g/2 oz butter
> ¹/4 cup/30 g/1 oz flour
> 2 cups/500 ml/16 fl oz
  milk
> ground white pepper

method

1. To make tomato sauce, heat oil in a frying pan
   over a medium heat, add mushrooms, onion,
   garlic and chili and cook, stirring, for
   5 minutes or until onion softens slightly. Stir
   in zucchini, tomatoes and wine and bring to the
   boil. Reduce heat and simmer for 15 minutes.
   Stir in basil and parsley and set aside.
2. To make spinach and ricotta sauce, mix all its
   ingredients in a bowl. Set aside.
3. To make white sauce, melt butter in a saucepan
   over a medium heat, stir in flour (a) and cook,
   stirring, for 1 minute. Remove from heat and
   whisk in milk (b). Return to heat and cook,
   stirring, for 5 minutes or until sauce boils and
   thickens (c). Season with white pepper.
4. To assemble, line base of a lightly greased
   ovenproof dish with one-third of the lasagna
   sheets, cutting to size as necessary. Top with
   half the tomato sauce, then half the
   remaining lasagna sheets, the remaining
   tomato sauce and remaining lasagna sheets.
5. Spread spinach and ricotta sauce over lasagna,
   pour over white sauce and sprinkle with tasty
   cheese (mature Cheddar). Bake at
   180°C/350°F/Gas 4 for 30-40 minutes or until
   mixture is hot and bubbling and top golden.

Serves 6

tip from the chef

*For easier serving, allow lasagna to stand in a warm
place for 20-30 minutes to settle before cutting.*

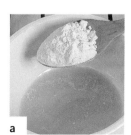

a

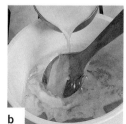

b

c

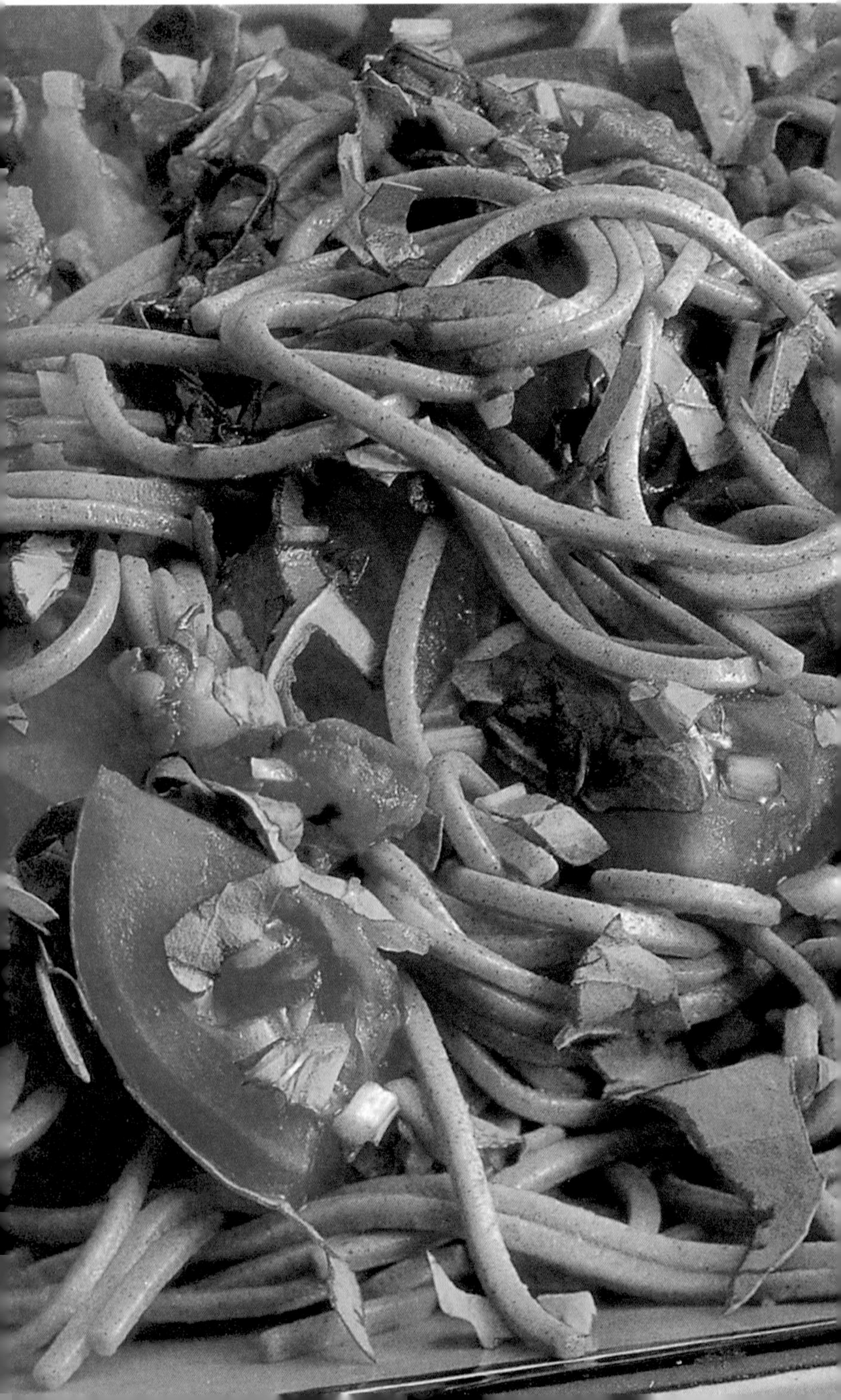

spicy buckwheat noodles

■□□ | Cooking time: 20 minutes - Preparation time: 10 minutes

method

1. Cook noodles in boiling water in a large saucepan following packet directions. Drain, set aside and keep warm.
2. Heat oil in a frying pan. Add garlic and cook, over a medium heat, stirring, for 1 minute. Add chilies, rocket and tomatoes and cook for 2 minutes longer or until rocket wilts. Toss vegetable mixture with noodles and serve immediately.

ingredients

> 500 g/1 lb buckwheat noodles
> 1 tablespoon olive oil
> 3 cloves garlic, crushed
> 2 fresh red chilies, seeded and chopped
> 200 g/6 1/2 oz rocket leaves, shredded
> 2 tomatoes, chopped

Serves 4

tip from the chef

If rocket is unavailable you can use watercress instead. For a complete meal, accompany with a tossed green salad and wholemeal bread rolls.

okra
and bean stew

■ ■ □ I Cooking time: 35 minutes - Preparation time: 30 minutes

ingredients

> 2 teaspoons vegetable oil
> 2 cloves garlic, crushed
> 2 fresh red chilies, chopped
> 2 onions, sliced
> 250 g/8 oz okra
> 2 eggplant, chopped
> 2 x 440 g/14 oz canned peeled tomatoes, undrained and mashed
> 440 g/14 oz canned red kidney beans, rinsed
> 250 g/8 oz firm tofu, cut into chunks
> 1/2 cup/125 ml/4 fl oz red wine
> 1 tablespoon brown sugar
> 3 tablespoons chopped fresh basil
> freshly ground black pepper

method

1. Heat oil in a large saucepan. Add garlic, chilies and onions and cook over a medium heat, stirring constantly, for 5 minutes or until onions are soft and golden.
2. Add okra, eggplant, tomatoes, beans, tofu, wine and sugar. Bring to the boil, then reduce heat and simmer for 30 minutes. Stir in basil and black pepper to taste.

....

Serves 4

tip from the chef

Serve this tasty vegetable stew with wholemeal pasta or brown rice.
When preparing fresh okra, wash it well and handle it carefully. Rub it gently under running water to remove the fuzzy outer layer.

vegetable chili

a

■■□ I Cooking time: 2 hours - Preparation time: 45 minutes

method

1. Sprinkle eggplant with salt. Stand for 15-20 minutes. Rinse under cold, running water and pat dry with absorbent paper.
2. Heat 1 tablespoon oil in a large frying pan and cook eggplant (a) until just tender. Set aside.
3. Heat remaining oil in a large casserole dish. Add onion, garlic and green pepper (b) and cook until onion softens. Stir in tomatoes, zucchini (c), chili powder, cumin, parsley, beans (d), eggplant and pepper to taste. Cook until heated through.
4. Bake at 180°C/350°F/Gas 4 for 1½ hours or until eggplant skin is tender and the casserole bubbling hot.

....
Serves 6

ingredients

> 1 large eggplant, cut into 1 cm/½ in cubes
> salt
> 4 tablespoons olive oil
> 1 large onion, chopped
> 1 clove garlic, crushed
> 1 green pepper, sliced
> 425 g/14 oz canned peeled tomatoes
> 2 zucchini, sliced
> 1 teaspoon hot chili powder
> ½ teaspoon ground cumin
> 4 sprigs fresh parsley, finely chopped
> 500 g/1lb canned three-bean mix
> freshly ground black pepper

tip from the chef

For an even lighter dish, steam all the vegetables in a Chinese bamboo steamer.

b

c

d

corn and
zucchini casserole

■□□ I Cooking time: 30 minutes - Preparation time: 20 minutes

ingredients
> 2¹/₂ cups cooked corn kernels, drained
> 4 zucchini, cut into slices
> 3 ripe tomatoes, chopped
> ¹/₂ cup tomato purée
> 1 large onion, peeled and chopped
> 1 red pepper, seeded and chopped
> 4 cups vegetable stock

method
1. In a large deep frying pan add corn, zucchini, tomatoes, tomato purée, onion and pepper, cook for 5 minutes over medium heat.
2. Add the stock and bring to the boil, reduce heat, simmer for 25 minutes. Serve hot.

....
Serves 6

tip from the chef
The combination of zucchini and corn is excellent. For variation, briefly boil zucchini and hollow out. Blend pulp with aromatic herbs, add corn kernels, combine with a beaten egg and fill hollowed zucchini. Sprinkle with grated cheese and bake.

index